George Reynolds, Joseph Hyrum Parry

The Mormon Metropolis

George Reynolds, Joseph Hyrum Parry

The Mormon Metropolis

ISBN/EAN: 9783337297886

Printed in Europe, USA, Canada, Australia, Japan

Cover: Foto ©Lupo / pixelio.de

More available books at **www.hansebooks.com**

THE

"MORMON" METROPOLIS:

AN

ILLUSTRATED GUIDE

——TO——

SALT LAKE CITY AND ITS ENVIRONS

Containing Illustrations and Descriptions of Principal
Places of Interest to Tourists; also Interesting
Information and Historical Data with
Regard to Utah and its People.

SALT LAKE CITY, UTAH:
J. H. PARRY & COMPANY, PUBLISHERS.
1889.

CONTENTS.

ℐLLUSTRATIONS.

THE "MORMON" METROPOLIS:

AN ILLUSTRATED GUIDE TO

Salt Lake City and its Environs.

INTRODUCTORY.

S IT is "MORMONISM" alone which gives to SALT LAKE CITY its unique pre-eminence among the cities of Western America, and that attracts the visits of the tourist and traveler, we shall in this brief but comprehensive GUIDE, give chief place to the edifices, etc. erected by this people, and the surrounding objects of interest associated with their eventful history.

The mercantile and manufacturing interests of this City will also be detailed, thus making this little work a handbook of reference for capitalists and business men, and all others interested in the commercial growth and development of the CITY OF SALT LAKE.

Unlike several of the surrounding Territories, which were settled by the Spaniards, and early became known to civilization, the Territory of Utah was almost entirely unknown before the advent of the "Mormon" Pioneers. In the summer of 1833, Captain Bonneville and a few trappers explored the northern part of Utah, including a portion of Salt Lake Valley, and Colonel J. C. Fremont spent four years—1842 to 46—exploring this region. With these exceptions, none but hunters and trappers had ever visited this inhospitable region, as it was then called. Heavy frosts prevailed every month in the year, and it was declared by old time trappers and hunters that the climate was so forbidding and the soil so barren, that no people could sustain themselves upon it. The whole basin was so barren as to produce little besides a species of bunch grass, and the ground was covered with myriads of large, black crickets, which constituted an article of food for some of the lower tribes of Indians. In Colorado, New Mexico and Arizona there are many evidences that civilized races once lived in those places and cultivated the soil. But there were no such evidences to be met with in the settlement of this valley. The advent of civilization was on the arrival of the "Mormon" Pioneers, after their expulsion from Nauvoo, Illinois.

On the 24th of July, 1847, President Brigham Young,* accompanied by 142 hardy Pioneers, emerged from the cañon on the east of the valley, which was at once named

---

*Brigham Young was born June 1, 1801, at Whittingham, Windsor County, Vermont; became a member of the Church of Jesus Christ of Latter-day Saints in 1832, ordained an apostle in 1835, and died in Salt Lake City, August 29, 1877.

Great Salt Lake City, 1863.

"Emigration Cañon," and may be recognized as the gorge immediately south of Fort Douglas, and entered into the Great Salt Lake Valley. They had left their homes in Illinois the year previous, spending the winter in camps on the Missouri River. As soon as the grass was high enough to sustain their cattle, they left their winter quarters and began their weary and perilous march through a hostile Indian country, seeking out, and making a new road of 650 miles, and following a trapper's trail nearly 400 miles over the Rockies, in order to find a new home for their followers. In less than a week the Pioneers were joined by a company of Saints from Mississippi, accompanied by Captain James Brown and a detachment of the "Mormon" Battalion who served their country in the war against Mexico.

Although late in the season, plowing and planting immediately began, as the people were already on short rations, and depending upon the products of the soil for future supplies. The ground was so thoroughly parched and baked that several plows were broken in the first efforts to subdue the soil. Ditches were dug from the mouth of City Creek Cañon and the whole of that stream was turned upon the community farm. Thus began, in Utah, the system of irrigation to which her wealth, beauty and productiveness are due almost wholly to-day. Without irrigation Utah would still remain the "barren desert" it was when visited by the early trappers; and the story of the "Mormons," by their industry "making the desert to blossom as the rose," would never have been written. Thus, Salt Lake City, the "Mormon" Metropolis, the most attractive and most promising city of western America, was founded.

Although this was then Mexican soil, the Stars and Stripes were unfurled, and the country was taken possession of in the name of the government of the United States.

Within a few weeks after their arrival, the colonists had built twenty-seven log cabins, laid out and built a fort for their protection against the savage Red Man; had nearly a hundred acres plowed and planted with potatoes, wheat, etc. Much of the crops were injured by early frosts, and in consequence much suffering and privation ensued, and the people were still kept on rations. To add to the scarcity, the emigrating Saints who arrived in the fall, some 700 wagons laden with families, brought scarcely any provisions. A company of the "Mormon" Battalion, which had been disbanded in California found their way here during the first winter, all destitute of provisions, yet none died of want. It has often been said that no other community could have provided so well against starvation. The unity of the people, guided and directed by their leaders, Brigham Young and others, preserved them from starvation. Those who had food willingly shared with those who were destitute. It was in these early days that President Young instituted the monthly fast day, that food might be saved and given to the poor. This practice is kept up to this day, and of late years nearly all the "Mormon" places of business are closed during the forenoon of the first Thursday of each month, that the employees may have opportunity to attend fast meeting and offer their donations to the poor.

In the spring of 1848 a great deal of ground was broken, and was planted with seed which had been saved; every care was taken to insure an abundant harvest. In the month of June, the black crickets, which the Pioneers had encountered the year before, came down from the hills in myriads, and threatened to entirely destroy the growing crops. They devoured everything before them, and as all the hope for bread was in the crops the prospects for the colonists were gloomy indeed. The people were powerless against this foe, and starvation seemed inevitable, when, to their great relief, immense flocks of sea gulls, suddenly appeared upon the scene and soon destroyed the crickets, and saved sufficient of the crops to keep the people from starvation. As these gulls were never seen in this region before, their appearance was acknowledged as a divine interposition of Providence in behalf of the people. As it was food was so scarce the ensuing winter that many were compelled to subsist upon raw hides, segoes and thistle roots.

The first postoffice in this city was opened in March, 1849, Joseph L. Heywood being the postmaster.

In the summer of 1849 parties from the east, on the way to the California gold mines, arrived. They brought with them all kinds of merchandise, wagons, tools, and farming implements, which they gladly disposed of in exchange for provisions. In this manner all kinds of commodities were sold as cheaply in Salt Lake City as in the cities of the east.

A provisional government was established, and a constitution adopted for the government of the new "State of Deseret," and A. W. Babbitt was sent to Congress asking for admission into the Union.

The Indians were at times very troublesome; outbreaks occurring frequently, caused principally by the unwise course pursued by travelers and gold seekers in giving

whiskey to them, sometimes quarreling with them and incit-
ing them to acts of violence.   Deeming it cheaper to feed the
Red Man than to fight him, the "Mormon" Indian policy
has been a peaceful one from the beginning. and as a result
there have been fewer Indian outbreaks in Utah than in any
other western Territory.

In Sept., 1850, the Territory of Utah was organized by
act of Congress, and Brigham Young was subsequently appointed Governor, and took the oath of office the February
following.   On January 11, 1851, Great Salt Lake City was
incorporated, with Jedediah M. Grant as Mayor.   On September 22, 1851, the first Legislature of Utah Territory con-
vened in Great Salt Lake City, and in the following November the University of Deseret was opened.

The population increased very rapidly each year.
"Mormon" immigrants arrived from all parts of the world.
They came by way of the Missouri River, thence by ox
teams and handcarts across the "plains."

The years of 1855-6 will long be remembered by the
early settlers as a period of scarcity and famine.   What
crops were not destroyed by drouth were eaten up by grasshoppers.   Many domestic animals died of starvation, and
food was so scarce that many families did not taste bread for
months at a time.   It was at this time that a species of yam
was discovered which served for potatoes.   This "provi-
dential root" was unknown before and has not been known
since the "grasshopper war" of the "hard times" of '55 56.
The harvest of 1857, however, was the best Utah had had
up to that time.

In the fall of 1857, Judge Drummond and others erroneously reported that troubles had arisen between the Territorial and United States officials, that the "Mormons" had risen in rebellion and had expelled all U. S. officials from the Territory. In consequence of this the "Utah Army" was sent under Colonel A. S. Johnston to settle the reported difficulties. Without making any investigation into the charges, which were afterward proven to be without any foundation, the Government sent an expedition against the people of Utah at an expense of nearly $40,000,000. In March, 1858, the citizens of Great Salt Lake City, and the settlements north of it, agreed to abandon their homes and "go south"—whence they knew not, except that they were again to follow their leader Brigham Young in exile. The people were under the impression that the approaching army was sent to destroy them. By the month of June, the newly appointed Governor, James Cumming, and the peace commissioners arrived and investigated matters. The misunderstanding was speedily adjusted. The army passed through the deserted city and located at Camp Floyd, in Cedar Valley, about forty miles south-west of Salt Lake City, and the people returned to their deserted homes and resumed their accustomed labors.

In the month of April, 1860, the first pony express arrived—from Sacramento in four days, from St Joseph, Mo., in six days.

In July, 1861, General Johnston with his detachment of troops was ordered to the States at the breaking out of the Civil War, and the equipments that had not been ordered destroyed by U. S. authority and surplus provisions of the United States Army in Utah, were disposed of at auction

1t Lake City from Capitol Hill.

It was estimated that $4,000,000 worth of goods were sold for less than $100,000.

In the same year connection was made with the "outside world" by telegraph.

Colonel P. E. Conner, with the California Volunteers, arrived on Oct. 20, 1862, and located at Camp Douglas, the present site of Fort Douglas.

In 1867-8 the myriads of grasshoppers again visited the Territory and the crops were almost total failures both years.

On Jan. 10, 1870, the last rail of the Utah Central Railroad was laid, and the last spike driven by President Brigham Young, in the presence of 15,000 people. This was the inauguration of a new era in the growth and commerce of the city and Territory. Hitherto, all importations had to be freighted a thousand miles by ox or mule teams, and all immigrants had to tramp this weary road over vast and arid plains and toilsome mountains. Since the advent of the railroad the city has made much progress and has developed very rapidly, until it is to-day acknowledged to be the prettiest and, in many respects, the most desirable city to live in on the continent.

In March, 1883, the Denver & Rio Grande Railway was completed between Salt Lake and Denver, and it is reported that two other roads are headed this way, which will give Salt Lake plenty of facilities for travel in all directions.

SALT LAKE CITY.

SALT LAKE CITY, the capital of Utah, occupies an important central position in the Territory, and is the me-

tropolis of the inter-mountain region.   Its latitude is 40° 46′,
longitude 112° 6′ West; and the variation of the magnetic
needle at the base meridian, as determined in October, 1878,
by the United States Coast Survey, is 16° 32′ East

   The city has an area of nearly 10,000 acres, and a population of about 30,000 inhabitants.   It is laid out, principally, in blocks or squares of ten acres each, the streets
running due to the cardinal points.   Each street is 132 feet
wide, including the sidewalks, which are sixteen and one half
feet in width.   The north-eastern part of the city is divided
into blocks of five acres each, with streets eighty feet wide·
Nearly all the streets are bordered with shade trees and
running brooks and the building lots are usually large
enough to afford ample room for buildings, gardens, or-
chards and ornamental grounds.   The foliage largely con-
ceals the houses in summer, giving the city the appearance
of an immense and lovely garden.

   The altitude of the city is 4,300 feet above sea level.
The climate is salubrious.   The mean summer temperature
is about 74°, but on account of the dry and rare atmosphere
it is not more oppressive than a mean several degrees higher
would be on the sea level.   Although the mercury often
reaches above 90° in July and August, sunstroke is almost
unknown; thunder storms are frequent, the nights are uni-
formly cool, and residents of the city who are obliged to
visit the East in the hot months are glad to get back again.

THE SACRED SQUARE.

   THE TEMPLE BLOCK is the Sacred Square of the Latter-day Saints and the central object of interest to tourists

visiting the city. It covers an area of ten acres, is surrounded by a high adobe wall, and contains the Temple, now in the course of erection, Tabernacle, Assembly Hall, the Endowment House, and the architects' office, and workshops of the men engaged in the construction of the Temple.

" MORMON " TEMPLES.

Not less than eight temples have been designated, and their sites consecrated, of which number five have been dedicated and ordinances administered therein — at Kirtland, Ohio; Nauvoo, Illinois; St. George, Logan, and Manti, Utah. The temple at Salt Lake City, is progressing rapidly towards completion.

The temple at Kirtland was 55x65 feet; the corner stones were laid July 22, 1833 This was built by donation and voluntary contribution, and was completed and dedicated March 27, 1836.

The corner stone for a temple at Far West, Missouri, was laid July 4 1838, with appropriate ceremony. Dimensions of building to be 110 feet long and 80 feet wide.

The temple at Nauvoo, Illinois, was about 128 feet long by 88 feet wide. The corner stones were laid on the 6th day of April, 1841. The building was erected by the tithing and free-will offerings of the people, and was so rapidly advanced that on the the 8th of November the same year the baptismal font was dedicated, and baptisms for the dead were administered. The building was finally dedicated with public services on Saturday and Sunday, the 2nd and 3rd of May, 1846. After the expulsion of the Saints from Illinois, this temple was destroyed by fire.

The temple at St. George, Utah, the site of which was dedicated and ground broken November 9, 1871, is 141 feet 8 inches long by 93 feet 4 inches wide; is 84 feet from ground to top of parapet. The basement is of volcanic rock, the upper part of red sandstone, and contains about 1,900 cords of rock, 1,000,000, feet of lumber, and cost about $800,000.

The Manti Temple site was dedicated and the ground broken by President Brigham Young, on April 25, 1877. The corner stones were laid April 14, 1879. Its size is 172x95 feet, and 82 feet to the square. Its eastern tower is 179 feet high, the western tower 169 feet high. This edifice stands on a hill, which had to be partly removed and required 2,400 cords of rock terrace to provide for its location. This temple was completed in May, 1888, and dedicated on the 21st day of the same month.

The site of the Logan Temple is situated on an elevation or table land in the eastern part of the city bearing that name. It was dedicated with prayer offered by Apostle Orson Pratt, May 18, 1877, and the ground was broken the same day. The corner stones were laid September 17, 1877. The building, including towers and buttresses, is 171 feet long by 95 in width, with a tower 30 feet square at each end, the eastern tower is 155 feet, and the western tower 143 feet in height, and 86 feet from the surface to top of battlements. This temple was completed and dedicated with appropriate ceremonies on the occasion of a General Conference of the Church being held there on May 17, 1884.

SALT LAKE TEMPLE.*

The length of this building now in course of erection, east

Abridged from description of the late T. O. Angell, chief architect and west, is 186 feet 6 inches, including towers, by 99 feet in width. On the east end there are three towers, and the same number also on the west.

The north and south walls are 8 feet thick, clear of pedestal, they stand upon a footing of 16 feet wall, on its bearing, which slopes 3 feet on each side to the height of 7 feet 6 inches. The footing of the towers rises to the same height as the side, and is one solid piece of masonry of rough ashlers.

The basement of the main building is divided into many rooms by walls, all having footings. The line of the basement floor is 25 inches above the top of the footing. Four inches above the earth on the east end will begin a promenade walk, from 11 to 22 feet wide, around the entire building, and is approached by stone steps on all sides.

The footings of the four corner towers are 26 feet square. These continue 16 feet 6 inches high, and come to the line of the base string course, which is 8 feet above the promenade walk. At this point the towers are reduced to 55 feet square; they then continue to the height of 38 feet, or the height of the second string course. At this point they are reduced to 23 feet square; they then continue 38 feet high, to the third string course. The string courses continue all around the building, except when separated by buttresses. These string courses are massive mouldings from solid blocks of stone.

The two east towers then rise 25 feet to a string course, or cornice. The two west towers rise 19 feet and come to their string course or cornice. The four towers then rise 9 feet to the top of battlements. These towers are cylindri-

cal, having 17 feet diameter inside, within which stairs as-
cend around a solid column 4 feet in diameter, allowing
landings at the various sections of the building. The
towers have each five ornamental windows on two sides,
above the basement.

Salt Lake Temple.

The two centre towers occupy the centre of the east and
west ends of the building, starting from their footings 31
feet square, and break off in sections in line with corner
towers to the height of the third string course. The east

centre tower then rises 40 feet to the top of battlements; the west centre tower rises 34 feet to the top of battlements. All the towers have ornamental spires surmounting them. The height of the east centre tower when completed will be 200 feet.

The center room of the basement is arranged for a baptismal font, and is 57 feet long by 35 feet wide, separated from the main wall by four rooms, two on each side.

The Temple site was consecrated and the ground broken for the foundation February 14, 1853. The corner stones were laid with imposing ceremonies on April 6, 1853.

The following inscription appears on a large tablet stone placed in the face of the east centre tower:

HOLINESS TO THE LORD.

THE HOUSE OF THE LORD,

BUILT BY THE

CHURCH OF JESUS CHRIST OF LATTER-DAY SAINTS.

COMMENCED APRIL 6, 1853.

COMPLETED:

. . . .

There have already been expended in its erection about $5,000,000, all of which has been voluntarily donated in tithing by the members of the "Mormon" Church. It is constructed of finely cut and finished granite rock, which is quarried from the mouth of Little Cottonwood Cañon, in the Wasatch range of mountains, some twenty miles to the south-east of the city.

At present, the government is in possession of the en-tire Temple Block, and the Latter-day Saints are paying rent to the United States government for the privilege o occupying and using their own houses of worship. This is in consequence of the construction put by the local Federal courts upon the recent act of Congress disincorporating the "Mormon" Church and escheating the property.

LARGE TABERNACLE.

It is well known that the site of SALT LAKE CITY was selected, the plotting of it designed, and the principal build-ings in it were planned, by President Brigham Young. The buildings he designed are remarkable for their substantial and convenient character. This peculiarity is very well illus-trated in the construction of the "New Tabernacle," as it has been called to distinguish it from the "Old Tabernacle," which formerly stood near it. This building is situated in the west centre of the Temple Block, and was commenced on the 26th of July, 1864, and was completed and dedicated October 6, 1867.

There is nothing very attractive about the outside ap-pearance of the building. To be appreciated it must be viewed from the inside. It is elliptical in shape, 250 feet long by 150 feet wide, and 70 feet in height from the floor to the ceiling at its highest part, or 80 feet from the floor to the top of the roof. The interior of the building presents an oval arch, without any centre support, the largest self-supporting arch in America, with the exception of that of the Central Depot, New York, and probably the largest in

THE TABERNACLE.

the world that is constructed wholly of wood. The bents
of the roof are composed of a lattice truss, aud rest upon
44 sand-stone pillars, each 3x9 feet in size, and from 14 to
20 feet in height. The gallery, which extends around the

The Tabernacle Crgan.

building, except at the west end, is 480 feet long by 30 fe t
in width.   The entire building has a seating capacity of
about 10,000.

It has 20 doors, most of which are 9 feet wide, and all open outward, so that an audience of 9,000 or 10,000 can gain egress, in case of emergency, in a very few minutes. In this respect the building is certainly without a rival in the world.

In the west end of the Tabernacle is situated the large organ, second to none in the United States in appearance and sweetness of tone, and is exceeded in size by but one. It was constructed entirely by Utah artizans, under the direction of Joseph Ridges, Esq. It has recently been entirely reconstructed by Niels Johnson, Esq., assisted by Mr. Henry Taylor.

To hear the melody of the organ richly repays a visit to the Tabernacle. The front towers of the organ have an altitude of 58 feet. The dimensions of the organ are 30x33 feet. The bellows are supplied with air by a water motor. The organ has 57 stops, contains a total of 2,648 pipes, ranging in length from 2 feet to 32 feet, distributed as follows: great organ, 840 pipes; swell organ, 728 pipes; choir organ, 504 pipes; solo organ, 336 pipes; pedal organ, 240 pipes; operated by 8 couplers and as many pedal movements.

SALT LAKE ASSEMBLY HALL.

The Salt Lake Assembly Hall, situated in the southwest cornor of the Temple Block, is perhaps one of the finest buildings used for public worship to be found in any of the western Territories. The late Obed Taylor, Esq., was the architect, and Henry Grow, Esq., its builder. It is constructed entirely of cut granite rock at a cost of $90,000, defrayed by voluntary contributions from members

of the "Mormon" Church in Salt Lake County, assisted
by the general funds of the Church. Its dimensions are 68
feet wide by 120 long, and is 130 feet to top of tower
rising from the centre of the building. It has a roof of 4
gables each surmounted with ornamental spires, as also are
the 4 corners of the Hall.

Salt Lake Assembly Hall.

There are 4 wide entrances, one on each side and end.
The same have stairways leading to the gallery.

The building is lighted with gas, and is heated in cold

weather by steam boilers, at a pressure of 1½ lbs. to the square inch.

A wide gallery extends around the entire hall, except at the west end, where the large organ is situated, and ample room is reserved for a choir of 100 singers. Immediately in front of the choir are three stands or pulpits, arranged conveniently in steps one above another, occupied by the leading authority of the church. In front of the stands is the sacramental table.

For its artistic design and many interesting historical reminiscences depicted upon it, the ceiling is worthy of special mention. It is divided into sixteen panels, of different shape and design, by an elegant moulding and border. Each panel is occupied by a beautiful fresco ornament, or painting representing historical scenes in the early rise of the Church, and paintings of the different temples built and now building by the Latter-day Saints. Representations of the Savior, Moses, Elijah, and Elias are also given. The two largest and principal panels are over the east and west ends of the Hall. That over the west end contains a fresco delineation of the All-Seeing Eye, and the emblematical Hive of Deseret, with the Kirkland and Nauvoo temples in the two lower corners. The panel over the east end contains a historical fresco painting of the angel "Moroni showing the Prophet Joseph where the plates were hid in the Hill Cumorah." The artistic fresco work of the ceiling was done by W. C. Morris, Esq.

The building was completed and dedicated in the spring of 1880.

The Hall will accomodate nearly 3,000 people. Its acoustic properties are perfect; an ordinary speaker can be heard distinctly at any part of the auditorium.

Regular Sunday services are held in the Large Tabernacle at 2 p. m.   Tourists and strangers are always welcome.

THE MUSEUM.

THE MUSEUM is situated on South Temple Stree, immediately facing the south entrance of the Temple Block. It should be visited by all who desire information with regard to the varied productions of Utah, and the number and importance of its advantages.   In this Museum may be seen specimens of native minerals, ores and manufactures, native animals, birds, reptiles and insects; wonderful fossils and petrifications; with many curiosities relating to the Indians of the Rocky Mountain region of old and modern times. The visitor to the Museum cabinets can get a better idea of the immense and varied resources of Utah, than by reading many books, or even visiting a few of its mines and manufactories.

The Museum is interesting also as showing what has been done by the "Mormon" people in the gradual development of manufactures and art.   Besides, there are rare curiosities from every part of the world —idols from Japan, China, the Sandwich Islands, etc.   A large collection of objects from Northern Europe, etc., and numerous curiosities gathered by missionaries in their proselyting travels.

One of the most interesting objects to visitors is the boat of Kit Carson, the first white man's vessel that plowed the waters of the Great Salt Lake.

The "Deseret News" Office.

SOUTH TEMPLE STREET.

LOOKING east from the southeast corner of the Temple Block, may be seen some of the most interesting of Salt Lake City's "old landmarks." At the corner opposite are the buildings of the

"DESERET NEWS" PUBLISHING COMPANY.

THE *Deseret News* is the oldest paper in the Rocky Mountains, and for years the only newspaper published between San Francisco and the Missouri river. Its first number appeared in June, 1850. It is the organ of the Church of Jesus Christ of Latter-day Saints. It possesses one of the largest and most substantial of paper mills in the west, sit. uated about fourteen miles southeast of the city; and has also a bindery and type foundry. It issues a Daily, Semi-Weekly and Weekly edition.

THE BISHOP'S GENERAL STOREHOUSE.

BEHIND the *Deseret News* building are the warehouses and yards of what were the General Tithing Store, now the store of the Presiding Bishop of the Church. It is the custom of the "Mormons" to pay their tithes and donations to the Church in kind. The farmer pays the products of his farm, the cattleman from the increase of his herds, the artizan and the laborer pays in "days' work." Consequently at the Tithing Store is gathered a most complicated assortment of products—grains, vegetables, merchandise, cattle, *ad infinitum.* These materials are paid out to the men who work on the temples, to the public hands and clerks, go toward the support of the poor, are doled out to friendly Indians, or exchanged for more available or desirable productions of the herd, farm, field or workshop.

A LITTLE over a half a block east of the *Deseret News* office stand the residences of the founder of SALT LAKE CITY— the late Brigham Young. The first is known as the Lion House, from the fact that a figure of a lion, crouch-

President Young's Residences.

ing, is placed over the front entrance. The Bee-Hive House is the next building to the east. A carved bee-hive (the insignia of Utah) crowns this edifice. Between these two houses are the offices of the Presidency of the "Mormon" Church. Here the Church dignitaries, when at home, receive such visitors as are properly introduced. In

these offices are also the head-quarters of the Deseret
Telegraph line, which has wires running to every settlement
of any importance in Utah Territory.

PRESIDENT YOUNG'S GRAVE.

PRESIDENT YOUNG'S grave is situated about a quarter of

President Young's Grave.

a mile north-east of the Eagle Gate, in an enclosure surrounded by an iron fence.

THE EAGLE GATE.

East of the Bee Hive House is the entrance to
City Creek Cañon. The high cobble wall formly con-
tinued uninterruptedly east. Here was situated the Eagle

Eagle Gate and Bee-Hive House.

Gate   The rock supports still remain, as an old landmark, with the artistically executed eagle perched on the summit. A short distance further east is another of President Young's residences, known as the White House, whilst to the north east is the building that he used for a school-house for his family.   It is occupied now by a portion of the Salt Lake Stake Academy.

THE GARDO HOUSE.

OPPOSITE the Bee-Hive House, south, is the Gardo House, the residence of the President of the "Mormon" Church.   It was built by Brigham Young, but not occupied permanently by him.   It is a very pleasing specimen of Utah architecture.

HISTORIAN'S OFFICE.

West of the Gardo House is the office of the Church Historian.   Here the historical records of the Church are kept, and copy preserved of all works, that can be obtained, which are written for or against the faith and practices of the society.

THE SOCIAL HALL.

HALF a block south of the Eagle Gate is the Social Hall.   It was the dramatic centre before the Theatre was built and is still used for balls, parties, children's exhibitions, assemblies, fancy fairs, etc.   Like the rest of the buildings erected by the late "Mormon" President, solidity rather than elegance characterizes its style of architecture. Old "Mormons," of Utah's early days, are never wearied telling of the good times experienced within its walls.   It is now used as a "Mormon" academy.

The Gardo House.

SALT LAKE THEATRE.

This imposing and massive edifice stands on the north-west corner of First East and First South Streets. It was erected at the instance and under the personal direction of the late President Brigham Young. It has undergone many improvements since his demise, and no pains are spared by its present proprietors to make it one of the best appointed in the West. It is a capacious building, 175 feet in length and 80 feet in width, and 60 feet from floor to ceiling inside, having a stage 65 feet deep and 32 feet at the proscenium, and it is fully supplied with traps, properties and scenery. It has a parquette, dress and three upper circles, and two private boxes each side of the proscenium. It will seat comfortably 1,500 persons. The outside presents an imposing appearance, granite finish on adobe walls, fluted columns, massive cornices in the simple Doric style of archi-tecture. The interior is decorated with taste, and when lighted up is very fine. The scenery is the production of the best artists, and looks so real that it commands the ad-miration of all spectators. In all its appointments the theatre is first class. The most talented actors in tragedy and comedy have trod its boards, and have been patronized with appreciation.

THE WALKER OPERA HOUSE.

In 1882 the Messers Walker Bros. erected this beauti-ful building, situated on Second South Street. It is a pleasing building on the exterior, with a very tasteful front. The interior is highly ornamented. It is 165 feet long, 67 feet wide and 60 feet from floor to ceiling. The stage is 48 feet deep by 59 feet broad. It has parquette, dress circle, two upper circles, and four private boxes, two each side of the proscenium.

THE CITY HALL.

THE City Hall, a red sandstone building, on First South Street, was erected at a cost of $70,000, It contains the offices of the Mayor, Recorder, Treasurer, Assessor and Collector, Water Master, and Chiefs of the Fire and Water Departments, the Alderman and Justice's court room and Council Chamber. For many years past the Territorial Legislative Assembly has held its bi-annual sessions in this building.

SALT LAKE CITY has had but seven mayors since its incorporation—Hons. Jedediah M. Grant, A. O. Smoot, Daniel H. Wells, Feramorz Little, Wm. Jennings, James Sharp, and Francis Armstrong, the last named being the present incumbent.

In the rear of the City Hall are the municipal prisons, built of cut stone, massively put together with an inch and a half bolt between each block, cemented together so that escape is very difficult.

THE FIRE DEPARTMENT.

EAST of the City Hall is the old building formerly used for the City Hall, when Salt Lake City was a very small burg. It is now occupied by the Fire Department and known as the Fireman's Hall.

Besides the engine room for the apparatus, on the ground floor of the Fireman's Hall, a large and well furnished room on the upper story affords ample space as a meeting room and bunk room, with accommodation for twelve or fourteen men, as well as library and reading room. The library now contains over 1,500 volumes, and has mainly been accumulated through the generosity of citizens interested in the welfare of the firemen.

The department at present numbers, officers and members, fifty men, including the chief engineer with the following apparatus: One Silsby steamer, two hand engines, five hose carts, one hook and ladder truck, with 5,400 feet of hose. Nine "Regulars" are paid $60 per month. The forty others are call men, who receive $50 a year each.

Col. G. M. Ottinger, formerly of Philadelphia, is the chief engineer of the Fire Department.

During the year 1887 there were 34 fires in the city limits, aggregating a total loss of $66, 265.

The average loss by fire in Salt Lake City is lower than in any other city of its size in the West.

STREET RAILWAY.

THE horse car accomodations of Salt Lake are ample to reach nearly every point of note in the city. At present, the lines are in the aggregate about 15 miles in extent. The system has been divided up so as to have through lines over 4 routes, which formerly were separated into 8 routes. All the depots and nearly all the hotels are reached by the street cars, also the following points—the Warm Springs Bath Houses, Liberty Park, the Eleventh Ward, adjoining Fort Douglas Military Reservation, the First, Sixth and Twenty-first Wards. The company employ 16 cars, 30 men, and 106 mules. The animals are required to do duty to the extent of about 16 miles per day, which only requires from 4 to 5 hours daily services.

Mr. O. P. Arnold is manager of the lines.   The capital invested aggregates $100,000.

THE WATER WORKS.

THE water supply for the city mains is obtained from City Creek, a cañon stream north of the city.   The flow of this stream at its best (during the month of June) is about 1,000,000 gallons per hour, but, like all mountain streams, is variable.   The water is taken from the creek by a flume to three distributing and filtering tanks, having a combined capacity of 300,000 gallons.   The elevation of these reservoirs above the north-east corner of the Temple Block, is 185 feet, and gives an average water pressure of 86 pounds to the inch.   The water is distributed at present through 24 miles of piping, varying in diameter from 20 to 3 inches.   On this line of mains are located 163 hydrants and 78 gates or valves, which supply 2,000 water-takers with an average daily consumption of water during the summer months, of nearly 8,000,000 gallons, and during the winter season of about 2,400,000.   During the past year extensive improvements have been made in the entire system of water works. A new plant has been made two miles higher up the cañon, which almost doubles the capacity and supplies an additional pressure of 36 pounds to the square inch, besides furnishing water to the "Dry Bench" in the north-east portion of the city.   Thus far   there has been expended $425,000 on the water works of this city, and from 1½ to 2 miles of extensions are added to the mains yearly.

The annual expenditures, exclusive of extensions, is about $6,000; the revenue about $30,000 per annum.

On MAIN (East Temple) Street, a little to the south of the Temple Block, stand the mammoth premises of Zion's Co-operative Mercantile Institution, familiarly known as the Big Co-op. This extensive establishment has branch houses in Provo, Ogden, and Logan (in Utah) and Soda Springs (Idaho); while numerous local retail "Co-op." establishments are to be found throughout the regions occupied by the "Mormons," in fact, nearly every settlement, large or small, has its co-operative store. Co-operation was a favorite subject with the late Brigham Young, and he was the founder of this Institution, and its first president. It was organized Oct. 16, 1868, and commenced business in March, 1869. To-day, it is one of the most solid mercantile firms in the world. Its business, last year, amounted to nearly $5,000,000.

The main building has a depth of 319 feet and a frontage of 98 feet. It has four stories including cellars. Its stock of goods at last stock-taking was valued at $1,500,000

Connected with Z. C. M. I. is the largest Boot and Shoe Manufactory between Chicago and San Francisco. The factory is situated on South Temple Street, a little east of Main, adjoining the main store of the institution. This branch of the business was established in 1879, and now employs 150 hands. In price, its products compete with goods manufactured elsewhere, and for quality are preferred by the Utonians to the imported article. Mr. W. H. Rowe is the superintendent and manager of this department, and Mr. D. M. McAllister, the secretary. Another branch of manufacture is associated with this factory, that of making overalls, jumpers and shirts, in which it successfully competes with San Francisco Chinese labor.

A tannery (established in the north-western portion of the city), into which many improvements have lately been introduced, is also connected with the manufacturing department of the Co-op. The total value of its yearly products is nearly $300,000.

The industries controlled by Z. C. M. I, in this city, employ 300 hands, constantly.

MANUFACTURING INDUSTRIES.

BESIDES the home industries sustained by Z. C. M. I. the city boasts of quite a number of manufacturing enterprises, chief among which are the Salt Lake Foundry and Machine Company's works, one block south of the Utah Central Railway depot, manufacturers of engines, boilers, etc. ; Davis, Howe & Co.'s Iron and Brass Foundry and Machine Shop, First West Street; the Silver Iron and Machine Works, North Temple Street; Haines & Sons, Boiler-Makers, South Temple Street; the Machine Shops of the Utah Central Railway Co., Locomotive and Car Builders, and J. W. Summerhays & Co., Leather Manufacturers. All the above institutions are constantly running to their utmost capacity, and turn out work second to none.

The furniture manufactory of Henry Dinwoodey is the oldest and largest of its kind in the territory, having been established in 1857. Mr. Dinwoodey keeps 31 employees very busy in his furniture making and upholstery departments.

Simon Bros. employ 10 hands in their Manufacturing Millinery Deparment.

Sam Levy, manufacturer of fine cigars, employs some 20 hands, and produces annually about 800,000 fine hand-made cigars. The business was first established in 1871, 5,000 cigars being made the first year.

Messrs. J. W. Summerhays & Co. are operating one of the finest tanneries in the West in the conversion of sheep skins into fine leathers, much of which are exported, and some of the finer grades are used in book-binding, in making children's fine shoes, etc.

The Salt Lake Glass Works, situated north-west of the city, are doing a very profitable business, and employ about 60 men and boys. The capacity of the works, including all the various sizes and kinds of bottles made, is nearly 600 dozen per day.

The Salt Lake Chemical Works, situated a short distance from the Glass Works, is another enterprise of considerable importance, although but recently begun. From native raw materials, which are to be had in abundance, the operators are turning out large quantities of refined soda, soda ash, sal soda, caustic soda, hypo-sulphate of soda, and Portland cement.

The Burton-Gardner Company occupy very extensive premises opposite the Theater, where is manufactured woven-wire bed mattresses and wire fencing. On the same street, a short distance south, are the premises of the Salt Lake Fence Co., another manufacturing establishment recently established.

Next in importance to Z. C. M. I., in the manufacture of boots and shoes, is the factory of the Messrs. Solomon

Bros. who employ 45 hands, and turn out 75 pairs of boots and shoes daily.

Messrs. J. C. Cutler & Bro. represent the Provo Woolen Mills and have a display of the finest assortment of woolen goods west of Chicago. This factory is the leading manufacturing industry of the Territory.

Elias Morris, Esq., besides being one of our leading builders and contractors, is extensively employed in manufacturing fire brick, tiles, cement piping and plaster paris of superior quality.

H. A. Tuckett is extensively engaged in manufacturing all kinds of candies; his brands of candies are very popular throughout the Territory, and his establishment one of the largest and most complete in the west.

The Deseret Woolen Mills, owned by Wm. Jennings' Sons, are giving employment to 40 hands in the manufacture of yarns, cloths, etc., and in the knitting department 20 girls are kept busy.

The Utah Soap Manufactory is fully employed and turns out large quantities of No. 1 soap annually.

Taylor, Romney, Armstrong Co., Salt Lake Building and Manufacturing Co., and the Sierra Nevada Lumber Association, are the leading manufacturers of doors, sash, mouldings, etc., besides doing a large building and contracting business.

The Messrs. Watson Bros. are one of the leading contracting and building firms of the city, besides doing considerable business as monumental stone cutters.

The Salt Lake Silk Factory manufactures a very excellent line of dress goods, handkerchiefs, etc.

The Deseret Woolen Mills.

In addition to the industries enumerated, there are successfully conducted vinegar works, basket and broom factories, cigar factories, breweries, confectioneries, demijohn works, salt refining, trunk, furniture, fence and mattress factories, etc., etc., giving employment in all to over 1,200 people, and sustenance to over 5,000.

While the mercantile business of the city is, perhaps, overcrowded, there is ample room for the profitable investment of much capital in manufacturing industries of various kinds. With the establishment of a few more factories, machine shops and the like, the city will be more sure of a steady growth both in population and commercial importance.

RAILROADS.

THE completion of the Union Pacific Railway, the last one hundred miles of which was done under contract of President Young, and its tributary, the Utah Central Railway (which was opened for traffic on January 10, 1870), was an important event to the business interests of Salt Lake City, and was the occasion of no little rejoicing in all circles. It was the inauguration of a new era in the growth and commerce of the city. Hitherto all the necessaries and comforts of life which could not be produced at home had to be freighted a thousand miles by ox or mule teams, and all those who migrated to this country in the early days of its settlement, came by the same conveyances, and sometimes new-comers made their way hither from the Missouri river in hand-cart trains. The journey occupied several months, and was a weary drag over vast and arid plains and toilsome mountains.

As soon as the Utah Central Railroad was completed into Salt Lake City, the Utah Southern road (now incorporated into the Utah Central system), was commenced and pushed its way through Utah, Juab, Millard and Beaver counties to Frisco, connecting by rail the most thrifty agricultural and mining districts of Southern Utah. This road is now being pushed through Nevada to Southern California. Transportation was thus afforded for the rich and abundant harvests of the valleys and the mineral wealth of the mountain gorges.

Work was commenced on the Salt Lake division of the Denver & Rio Grande Railway (narrow gauge) late in the season of 1881, was pushed forward with the zeal characteristic of its management, and through connection was made between Salt Lake and Denver on the 30th day of March, 1883, and shortly after was extended to Ogden, and connection made with the Central Pacific Railway to California. This road traverses the fertile counties of Emery, Utah, Salt Lake, Davis and Weber, and is considered by travelers the most picturesque route east. This road has added very materially to the prosperity and growth of the Territory.

HOTELS.

The city is well provided with first-class hotel accommodations, the principal houses being the Cullen, Walker, Continental and Metropolitan; the Valley House, Clift House, White House and Spencer House also offer first-class accommodations to tourists and visitors, and at reasonable rates.

WARM SPRINGS BATH HOUSES.

THE Warm Sulphur Springs, situated in the extreme north-west of the city, are justly celebrated for their medicinal properties, many invalid tourists visiting SALT LAKE CITY for the special purpose of being benefited by the pleasant and renovating baths to be had in its tepid waters. The bath houses are reached by street cars from the Eagle Emporium.

PLEASURE RESORTS.

LIBERTY PARK, situated in the south-east suburbs, and reached by street car line, is a most pleasant and healthy place to visit during the summer months. It was laid out originally by the late President Young, and called the "Forest Farm." There are pleasant drives and walks, beautifully and abundantly shaded by native forest trees.

"Calder's Farm," about 3 miles south of town, is another suburban pleasure resort, provided with boats, swings, dancing floors, games, etc., incidental to such places.

"Washington Square," between First and Second East Streets, is the chartered ground of the Olympic Club of this city, and on gala days is the scene of bicycle and foot races, base ball and cricket matches, and other games and amusements.

"Fuller's Hill," in the Tenth Ward, is another pleasure resort of considerable attraction, and is well patronized by the public.

FORT DOUGLAS.

ONE of the most interesting points in the vicinity is Fort Douglas, a well built, full-regiment post, located on a plateau about 3 miles east of and 500 feet above the city.

Garfield Beach, Great Salt Lake.

The post and grounds are laid out with taste, a small stream of mountain water making the culture of trees, shrubbery, grass and flowers possible. The elevation gives almost a bird's-eye view of the city and valley. In the distance lies the Dead Sea of America, a blue band drawn along the base of island mountains, the vistas between which are closed by more distant ranges. In the north, the Promontory divides the waters, ending far out in the lake. Across Jordan Valley the Oquirrh rises to a lofty height, white with snow a great part of the year, and often veiled by clouds. On the south, low hills appearing to be thrown out in echelon, complete the enclosure of Jordan Valley, which lies an unrolled map at one's feet.

The Salt Lake and Fort Douglas Railway runs several trains daily making street car connections at Liberty Park, First South and Twelfth East Streets.

ENSIGN PEAK.

To SEE the city at its best, one must climb to the rock-crowned summit of Ensign Peak. (So called from the circumstance of the "Mormons" almost immediately upon their arrival, erecting the National Flag on its apex, typical of their fidelity to the common-wealth, and emblematic of freedom to all mankind.) This dome-like mountain rises directly back of the town, and from it one may look down upon houses, trees and green squares. At the right lies the lake, dull hued, motionless and passive amid its grand surroundings. Huge islands of rock dot its surface, but no signs of life are to be seen. To the south stretches the beautiful valley, mountain guarded, fertile and bathed at its

Black Rock, Great Salt Lake.

lower end in a thin blue veil of haze. To the east is Fort Douglas, and beyond that Emigration Cañon.

The plateau immediately at the foot of Ensign peak, or between it and the city, has long been known as Arsenal Hill, part of which was recently given by the city to the Territory for Capitol grounds, and upon which will soon be built the Territorial Capitol. The remainder of this beautiful site is set apart for a public park. The cañon directly beneath on the east, is City Creek Cañon, the principal source of water for the City of the Saints. In it are situated the reservoirs of the Municipal Water Works. The scenery a short distance up the cañon is very beautiful, wild and romantic.

A nearer point at which to get a fine view of the city, is from Prospect Hill, located about half a mile north-east of the Eagle Gate. The beautiful view to be obtained from this point is well worth the travel to obtain it. Recently a fine tower has been built at this point for the accommodation of tourists.

SALT LAKE BATHING RESORTS.

GARFIELD BEACH, 20 miles west of the city on the shores of the Great Salt Lake, is reached by the Utah & Nevada Railway. During the summer season several trains run daily to this bathing resort.

Lake Park, a beautifully laid out pleasure and bathing place on the edge of the Great Salt Lake, is situated about 20 miles north of the city, and is reached by the Denver & Rio Grande Railway. Several trains run daily to this point during the bathing season. No tourist should miss the op-

Toyo Park Bathing Resort.

portunity thus afforded of taking a bath in the buoyant waters of the lake.

In the long sunny days of June, July and August, the water becomes deliciously warm, and it is much warmer than ocean water a month earlier and later.

Ample accommodations are afforded the visitors to make a few days' stay at these points, a rare opportunity to invalids, who would be benefited much by a short sojourn not only from the bathing, but by breathing the cool saline air of the lake.

The water of the lake contains 22 per cent. of pure salt, making it so buoyant that the least possible effort is necessary to keep one's equilibrium, as sinking is out of the question. Care, however, must be taken that the water is not inhaled into the mouth and nostrils, lest the bather is strangled.   ·

TERRITORIAL EXPOSITION BUILDING.

THIS building, now in course of erection, is situated in the centre of what is known as the Tenth Ward Square, a ten-acre block in the eastern part of the city. It measures 94 feet on the east and west line by 143 feet on the north and south line, exclusive of a principal entrance on the west and a wing 40x70 feet on the east. Stretching to the north and south of the centre building are two wings forty feet wide and one story high. The main building is two stories, with four towers. Each of these wings ends in a two-story building, from which other wings extend east and

west, giving a frontage of 294 feet on either end. Thus
the whole is intended for a grand structure stretching

Territorial Exposition Building.

through the centre of the block, from north to south, a distance of 620 feet. The highest point, exclusive of the pole
or staff, is 120 feet above the first floor.

THE CITY OF SALT LAKE is well provided with good churches, if we consider the number of citizens not connected with the "Mormon" Church.

St. Mark's Church.— Sixteen years ago St. Mark's Episcopal Church was established in this city by Bishop D. S. Tuttle, the bishop of this diocese. St. Mark's Parish includes St. Paul's Chapel under its administration. The Bishop is at the head of the Cathedral Parish, with three assistant ministers: the Rev. Messrs. N. F. Putnam, G. D. B. Miller and C. M. Armstrong. The Cathedral is located on First South Street, between Second and Third East Streets. It is built of red sandstone, quarried in a cañon near the city. It consists of nave and one transept. The architecture is Gothic. The nave was erected in 1870, and the transept was added in the summer of 1882. The transept is occupied by the organ and choir. The organ, which was put in its place in December, 1882, is one of the best in the West. Its tones are pure and sweet, and fill the church. The rectory is next door to the church. This and the lot on which it stands, was purchased by the congregation in 1887. The basement of the church is used for Sabbath school, and also for a day school in the primary department. Rev. N. F. Putnam, late of Peekskill, New York, is the present pastor of St. Mark's congregation.

St. Paul's Episcopal is also a stone structure and is well adapted to the wants of the membership; the congregation is presided over by Rev. C. M. Armstrong, who succeeded Rev. S. Unsworth, the first pastor of the church.

The Swedish Lutheran Church.—This neat church edifice is situated at the corner of Second South and Fourth

East Streets. The Lutheran mission was begun in 1882, and the church building was erected in 1885 at a cost of $10,000. Its dimensions are 66 feet long and 44 feet wide, and has a spacious basement, used at present for school purposes. The audience room of the church is one of the neatest in the city. The Rev. J. A. Krantz is the pastor of the church.

St. Mark's Episcopal Church.

St. Paul's Episcopal Church and Rectory.

Residence of John McDonald, Esq.

A. ZEESE & CO, Chi.

Methodist Church. — One of the finest church buildings, in size and architectural appearance, in the city, is the First Methodist Church, a brick structure of modern style. Rev. T. C. Iliff is the present pastor, and also has supervision over all the Methodist charges in Utah.

Presbyterian Church.— Rev. R. G. McNeice is the pastor of the Presbyterian Church. The church building is

The Swedish Lutheran Church.

on the corner with a street on the west and south. In the centre is the "Octagon," now used in connection with the boarding department of the Salt Lake Collegiate Institute.

Catholic Church.— The Catholic Church has a good chapel, and besides this, services are held in the chapel at the Hospital of the Holy Cross, and also at St. Mary's Ac-

The Catholic Hospital.

ademy, and at the chapel of All Hallow's College. Bishop Scanlan has supervision of the work in this city, and is aided by Fathers Keily and Blake.

Baptist.—The Baptists have a very fine church edifice on the corner opposite the County Court House, on Second South Street, and have a small congregation.

Jewish Synagogue.— The Jewish congregation is composed of some 50 members, presided over by M. C. Phillips. They have a commodious Synagogue, which is also used for school purposes.

SCHOOLS.

SALT LAKE CITY is divided into 21 school districts, in each of which a common school is maintained 10 months in

All Hallow's College.

each year. These schools are partly sustained by taxes and partly by tuition fees. All the branches of a common school education are taught by competent and interested teachers.

Besides the district schools, the city boasts of quite a

number of private institutions of learning and church schools, maintained by the various religious societies of the city, chief among which may be mentioned the schools of Hammond Hall (Congregational), Rowland Hall and St. Mark's School (Episcopal), the Salt Lake Collegiate Institute (Presbyterian) and the Hebrew school.

St. Mark's school, under the auspices of the Protestant Episcopal Church, was opened in 1857. It is a graded school with about 400 pupils and 12 teachers, having Primary, Grammar School, High School and Classical departments.

Rowland Hall, a boarding school for girls, opened in 1871. Here are 115 pupils and 8 teachers. The school has a full Academic Course of study, with superior opportunities for music, modern languages, drawing and painting.

The Deseret University, situated on Second West and First North Streets, under the management of Dr. John R. Park and an able and efficient corps of assistants, is the leading educational institution of the city and Territory. All the higher and many of the technical branches of education are here taught. It numbers among its students the youth of both sexes from all parts of the Territory; and some from Idaho and Arizona. One of its special features is the Normal department, for the training of teachers for the common schools of the Territory. A Deaf and Dumb Institute, liberal provisions for which were made by the last Territorial Legislature, will soon be built upon the adjoining grounds of the University. This department is at present under the very efficient management of Prof. Harry C. White.

The public school system of the city and Territory is

The University of Deseret.

but yet in its infancy.   No aid has been received from public funds, or other sources, for its maintenance, and until
very recently teachers were paid entirely by tuition fees, and
the schoolhouses built by subscription.   Schools have, however, been maintained in most of the city districts almost
continuously since the first settlement of the Territory, the
results of which are very gratifying, as very few of the children born here cannot read or write.

According to the educational statistics given in the
census for 1880, the percentage of illiteracy in Utah is
much below the average, and below more than half of the
States and Territories of the Union, and the percentage
about on a par with the great State of Massachusetts, not-
withstanding the unlimited educational facilities of the
latter.

In respect to the amount per capita of her school population which Utah has invested in school property, she stands
at the head of many older and more wealthy and populous
States, and not far behind some of the foremost States of
the Union, with an investment per capita of $8; while North
Carolina has invested less than 55 cents; Georgia, $2.03;
Kentucky less than $4; Virginia, $2. 55; Oregon, $5; Wis-
consin, $13.03; Minnesota, $14.55; Delaware, $10 35.

When it is remembered that in nearly every State in the
Union, vast sums of money derived from the sale of lands
or from the establishment of special funds, are devoted to
school purposes, and that these sums amount to tens and
hundreds of thousands of dollars annually, in many of the
States, while the schools of Utah have never yet received
any assistance whatever in this manner, the fact that she

Residence of Ex-Mayor James Sharp.

occupies her present advanced position in respect to education speaks volumes in her praise.

MUNICIPAL GOVERNMENT.

THE government of SALT LAKE CITY is one of the
best conducted and most economical in the United States.
The municipal expenditures, including salaries of all its officers, the maintainance of the police and fire departments,
and water works of the city, amounts to only $52,000 per
annum.   In consequence, taxes are extremely light, and the
machinery of government is so smoothly run that were it
not for occasional (biennial) elections, her citizens might for-
get they were not dwelling in a paradisiacal government.

Salt Lake City boasts of some 30,000 inhabitants, ard
has a police force of 15 men, including the city marshal,
one police officer to every 2,000 inhabitants.   The insignifi-
cance of this number may be inferred when compared with
other cities of the world.   In 1883 Philadelphia had one
police officer to every 636 of its citizens; New York, one to
every 562; Baltimore one to 525; Boston one to 487; the
metropolitian district of London, one to 342.   Yet notwith-
standing this great disparagement in the number of her police officers, life and property are infinitely safer than in any
of the cities named, and there is less crime in proportion to
the number of inhabitants than anywhere else in the world.
The quietness of her streets, and the absence of street fights,
riots and other public disturbances is proverbial.   The
quietness of the Sabbath day is particularly noticeable; all
business is suspended, there are no pleasure resorts of any
kind kept open, there is not the horse-racing, betting or

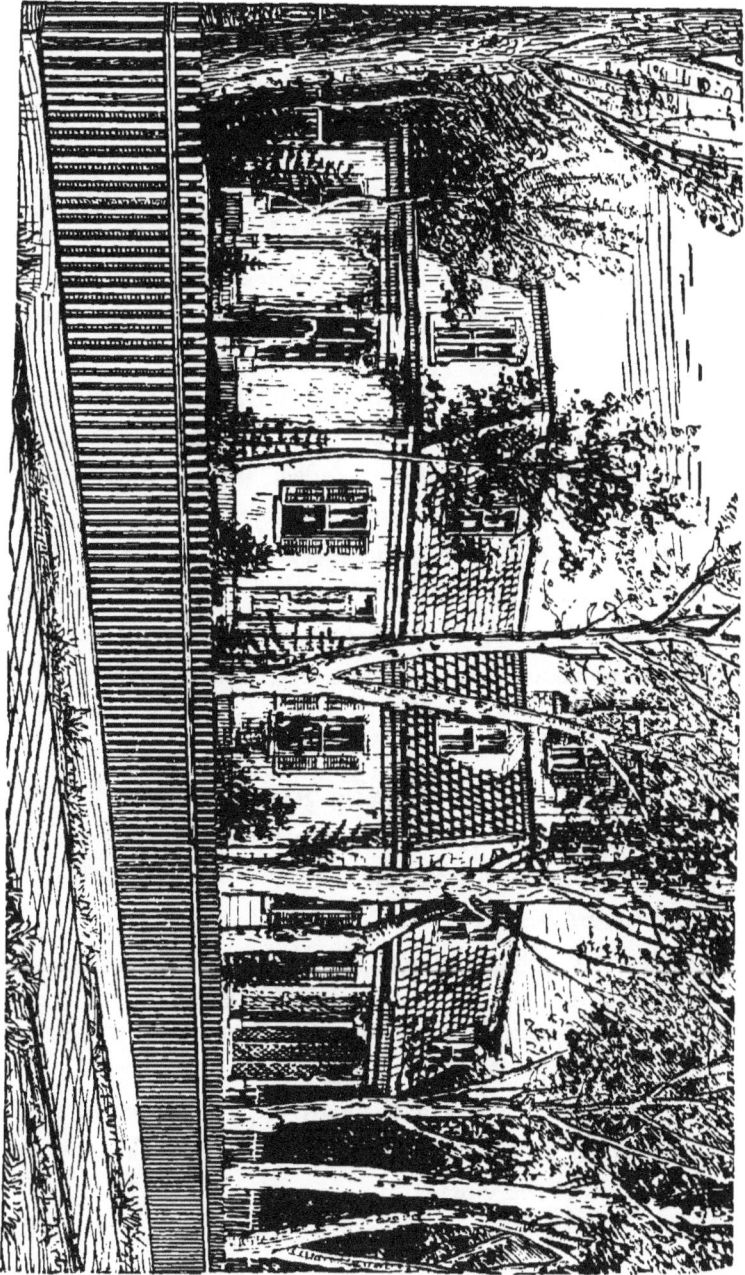

Suburban Residence of Col. J. R. Winder.

gambling on this day, that is met with in all other western towns, but the day is observed by all classes as a day of rest.

The Great Salt Lake, after which the city is named is 80 miles long and 40 miles wide, has seven islands, three of which are mountainous, and are used for grazing. Its nearest accessible point is some 15 miles north-west from Salt Lake City.

The river Jordan, the outlet of Utah Lake, pursues a very meandering detail course, but has a very direct general northerly course of some 40 miles, and empties into the Salt Lake about 10 miles from the city.

Utah Lake is a beautiful sheet of fresh water with an extreme length and breadth of 35 by 15 miles. It receives Provo and Spanish Fork rivers, and several other tributaries, and abounds in mountain trout and other fish.

CONCLUSION.

As MOST tourists who visit SALT LAKE CITY will be more or less interested in the people who built it, we close this little volume with the *Articles of Faith of the Church of Jesus Christ of Latter-day Saints:*

1.   We believe in God, the Eternal Father, and in His Son, Jesus Christ, and in the Holy Ghost.

2.   We believe that men will be punished for their own sins, and not for Adam's transgression.

3.   We believe that through the atonement of Christ all mankind may be saved, by obedience to the laws and ordinances of the Gospel.

4.   We believe that these ordinances are: first, Faith in

the Lord Jesus Christ; second, Repentance; third, Baptism by immersion for the remission of sins; fourth, Laying on of hands for the Gift of the Holy Ghost.

5. We believe that a man must be called of God by "prophecy and by the laying on of hands," by those who are in authority, to preach the Gospel and administer in the ordinances thereof.

6. We believe in the same organization that existed in the primitive church, viz: apostles, prophets, pastors, teachers, evangelists, etc.

7. We believe in the gift of tongues, prophecy, revelation, visions, healing, interpretation of tongues, etc.

8. We believe the Bible to be the word of God as far as it is translated correctly; we also believe the Book of Mormon to be the Word of God.

9. We believe all that God has revealed, all that He does now reveal, and we believe that He will yet reveal many great and important things pertaining to the Kingdom of God.

10. We believe in the literal gathering of Israel, and in the restoration of the Ten Tribes. That Zion will be built upon this continent. That Christ will reign personally upon the earth, and that the earth will be renewed and receive its paradisaical glory.

11. We claim the privilege of worshiping Almighty God according to the dictates of our own conscience, and allow all men the same privilege, let them worship how, where or what they may.

12. We believe in being subject to kings, presidents,

rulers and magistrates, in obeying, honoring and sustaining the law.

13.   We believe in being honest, true, chaste, benevolent, virtuous, and in doing good to *all men*; indeed we may say that we follow the admonition of Paul, "We believe all things, we hope all things," we have endured many things and hope to be able to endure all things.   If there is anything virtuous, lovely or of good report, or praiseworthy, we seek after these things.   JOSEPH SMITH.

www.ingramcontent.com/pod-product-compliance
Lightning Source LLC
Chambersburg PA
CBHW021514090426
42739CB00007B/606